*The Grosset & Dunlap
Read Aloud Library*

This book belongs to

The Grosset & Dunlap Read Aloud Library

BIBLE STORIES
From the New Testament

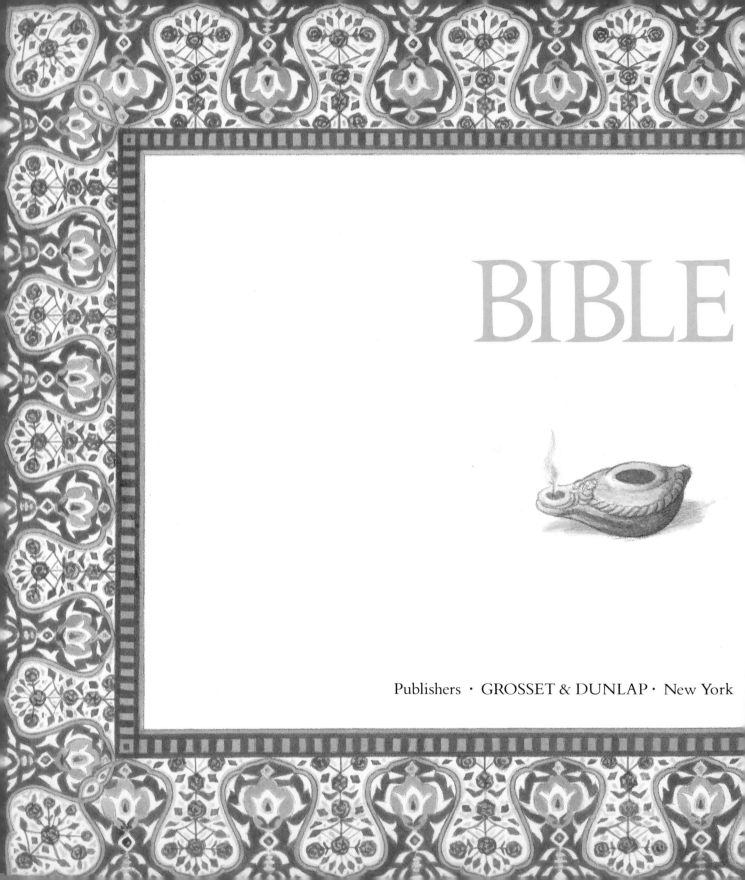

BIBLE

Publishers · GROSSET & DUNLAP · New York

STORIES
From the New Testament

Retold by Margaret Hopkins
Illustrated by Katherine Dietz Coville

A member of The Putnam Publishing Group

For my brother Ken, who always got there first,
and for Joshua, sweet Joshua.

K. D. C.

CONSULTANTS

Randall H. Balmer, Assistant Professor of Religion, Columbia University, New York
Steve Kinnard, Evangelist, The New York City Church of Christ, New York
Rev. Ledlie I. Laughlin, Jr., Rector, The Church of Saint Luke in the Fields, New York

Copyright © 1989 by Margaret Hopkins.
Illustrations copyright © 1989 by Katherine Dietz Coville.
All rights reserved.
Published by Grosset & Dunlap, a member of The Putnam Publishing Group, New York.
Published simultaneously in Canada. Printed and bound in Singapore.
Library of Congress Catalog Card Number: 87-83483   ISBN 0-448-19184-9
A B C D E F G H I J

CONTENTS

PROPHETS OF OLD

In ancient times, the people of Israel sometimes suffered hardship and sorrow. Then God sent prophets among them to tell the people of good things that lay ahead.

Again and again the prophets told the people about a promise God had made. The promise was that a Messiah, or Savior, would someday come among them and bring the light of God to the world. The Savior would be named Immanuel, which means *God with us*, and he would come from the family of David the king.

> For unto us a child is born, unto us a son is given;
> And the government shall be upon his shoulders;
> And his name shall be called Wonderful,
> Counsellor, the mighty God, the everlasting Father,
> the Prince of Peace.
>
> ISAIAH

> And you, Bethlehem in Judea,
> small as you are,
> out of you shall come Israel's ruler.
> He will appear and be their shepherd
> in the strength of the Lord.
> His greatness shall reach
> to the ends of the earth,
> and he shall be a man of peace.
>
> MICAH

THE BIRTH OF CHRIST

Long ago in the land of Israel, a young woman named Mary lived in the city of Nazareth in Galilee. She was engaged to a carpenter by the name of Joseph, who belonged to the ancient family of King David.

The Lord sent the angel Gabriel to Mary with a message. When Mary saw God's angel, she was frightened. "Fear not, Mary," said the angel, "for you have found favor with God. You are to have a son, and you will call him Jesus, which means Savior.

"He will be great and will be called the Son of the Highest," said the angel. "He will rule forever and his kingdom will never end."

Mary wondered at the news. "How can this be?" she asked. "I am not yet married."

And the angel answered, "The Holy Spirit will come upon you, and the power of the Most High will be with you."

Mary asked no more questions. "I am a servant of the Lord," she said. "Let it be as you have spoken."

Then the angel went away. Afterward Mary learned that what the angel had said was true. She was going to have a child.

Joseph, the man she was to marry, had a dream about the child. When he woke up from the dream, Joseph understood that the baby Mary would bear was sent by God. Then Mary became Joseph's wife, and they waited in Nazareth together for the child to be born.

In those days the land of Israel was ruled by the Romans.
A decree went out from the Roman emperor, Caesar Augustus,
that everyone in the empire must go to the city of his forefathers
to place his name on the taxpayers' lists.

Everyone went to register his name, each to the city of his
forefathers. Joseph and Mary left Nazareth and made the
journey down to the province of Judea. Joseph belonged to the
family of David, and so they travelled to Bethlehem, the city
where David had been born.

While in Bethlehem, the time came for Mary to have her
baby. She and Joseph had to stay in a stable because there was
no room in the inn. When her son was born, she wrapped him
in swaddling clothes. Then she laid him in a manger.

In the hills outside the town, shepherds were keeping watch over their flock by night. Suddenly an angel of the Lord appeared to the shepherds. The light of the Lord shone all around them, and the shepherds were afraid.

But the angel said to them, "Fear not, for I bring you news of great joy that will be for all people. A child has been born for you this day in the City of David. He is the Savior. He is Christ the Lord.

"You will know the child by this sign. He is wrapped in swaddling clothes and lies in a manger."

Suddenly there were many angels, all praising God and saying, "Glory to God in the highest. And on earth, peace, good will toward men."

When the angels had gone away, the shepherds told each other that they must go to Bethlehem. They had to see the child that had been announced to them by the angel.

The shepherds hurried to Bethlehem and found Mary and Joseph. And there was the baby, lying in a manger. Then the shepherds praised God for all the things they had heard and seen that night.

Later, wise men from the East went to find the child. They wanted to worship the one who had been born the Savior.

The prophets of old had said the Savior would be born in Bethlehem, so the wise men travelled to that city. The bright star they had seen in the East went before them, until it stood over the place where the child lay.

The wise men went in and saw the child with Mary, his mother. They fell to their knees and worshipped him. They brought out treasures and gave the child gifts of gold, frankincense, and myrrh.

After they had seen him, the wise men returned to their own country, far away.

MATTHEW and LUKE

13

THE FLIGHT INTO EGYPT

Mary called the baby Jesus, which was the name the angel Gabriel had told her to use. At the time of Jesus' birth, Herod was king of Judea. When Herod learned that a child born in his province would become a king one day, he was furious and wanted to destroy the baby.

The king ordered his soldiers to go to Bethlehem where the child had been born, and kill all the children there under three years old.

But God sent an angel to Joseph in a dream to warn him about King Herod. The angel told Joseph to take Mary and the baby and escape to the land of Egypt.

Joseph began the long journey that very night. He took the child and Mary away from Bethlehem and travelled to Egypt, where they were safe.

Time passed, and Joseph had a dream in Egypt. An angel told him that Herod had died and that Joseph and his family should leave Egypt and return to Israel. So Joseph took Mary and the little boy back to the place where Mary and Joseph had lived, to Nazareth in Galilee.

In that way an ancient prophecy was fulfilled. For the prophets had said: He that is the Messiah shall be called a Nazarene.

MATTHEW

JESUS IS BAPTIZED

There was rough, wild country in parts of Judea. In that wilderness, a young man called John the Baptist began preaching. He urged people to get ready for the Messiah who would soon be with them. He told people to turn to God and ask forgiveness for their wrongdoings.

Crowds came from all over Judea to listen to John. Many confessed their sins and were baptized by him in the Jordan River.

"I can baptize you with water," John said. "But there is someone coming after me who will baptize you with the Holy Spirit from God."

Soon the time came for Jesus, who had grown to manhood, to leave his home in Galilee and go to the banks of the Jordan River in Judea to be baptized by John.

When John saw Jesus, he knew that this was the one sent by God. Jesus asked John to baptize him, but John would not. "It is you who should baptize me," John said.

Jesus answered, "It is God's will that you do this." Then John agreed and baptized him.

Suddenly heaven itself opened above them. The Spirit of God came down to Jesus in the form of a dove. And a voice from heaven said, "This is my Son, whom I love. With him I am well pleased."

MATTHEW

THE TEMPTATION
IN THE WILDERNESS

After Jesus was baptized, he went into the desert by himself. For forty days and nights, he did not eat.

Then the devil, also called Satan, appeared. He began to tempt Jesus. "If you are the Son of God," Satan said, "turn the stones on the ground into bread."

"No," said Jesus. "The sacred scriptures, which are from God, say that man cannot live on bread alone. He needs the word of God to feed his soul."

Then Satan took Jesus to Jerusalem, high up on the rooftop of the temple. "If you are the Son of God," Satan said, "throw yourself off this high place. God's angels will catch you."

"No," said Jesus. "The scriptures say: Do not put the Lord your God to any test."

Then Satan took Jesus up on a mountain and showed him the kingdoms of the world. "I can give you power over all these," said Satan, "if you will bow down to me."

"Go away, Satan," said Jesus. "The scriptures say: Worship no one but the Lord your God."

Then Satan left Jesus by himself. Angels came and surrounded the Son of God and took care of him.

MATTHEW

19

Jesus Chooses His First Disciples

When Jesus came out of the desert, he began teaching about God the Father and eternal life in the kingdom of heaven. He went from town to town in Galilee, and he spoke with such power and grace that crowds gathered wherever he went.

One day a large crowd was listening to him on the shores of the Sea of Galilee. Little by little, people pressed forward to try to get closer to him. At last Jesus climbed into a nearby boat, one that belonged to a fisherman named Simon. Jesus sat in the boat a little way from the shore and went on teaching.

When he finished, Jesus told Simon and the other fishermen to sail out into deep water and lower their nets. Simon doubted

if they would catch anything and said, "Master, we have worked hard all night and have not caught a single fish. But I will do as you say."

The nets were lowered. Before long, Simon and the others began hauling in huge numbers of fish.

Simon was amazed by the size of the catch and astonished by what he had witnessed. He knelt before Jesus and asked to be forgiven for doubting him. In a nearby boat, two other fishermen, James and John, were filled with wonder and fear.

"Do not be afraid," said Jesus. "Follow me and I will make you fishers of men."

After they brought their boats to shore that day, the three men left everything behind them and followed Jesus. They became his disciples. Later Jesus gave Simon the name Peter.

LUKE

THE WEDDING IN CANA

Soon after Jesus began his teachings, there was a wedding in the town of Cana in Galilee. Mary, the mother of Jesus, attended the wedding feast. Jesus and his disciples went to the celebration also. It was a joyful event that lasted several days.

Before the feast was over, Mary learned that the wine for the guests had run out. She went to Jesus and told him there was no more.

At first, Jesus did nothing to answer his mother. It was not time yet for his power to be made known to many people. But at last he set about to solve the problem.

There were six large stone jars at the feast. Jesus quietly told the servants to fill the jars with water, which they did. Then he told them to pour some out and offer it to the master of the banquet.

The water in the jars had turned to wine. The banquet master tasted the wine and was amazed at its fine quality. Then he congratulated the bridegroom. "Most people serve their best wine first," he said. "After the guests have drunk well, then the host serves the less good wine and hopes no one will notice. But you have not done this. You have saved the best until last."

The bridegroom was pleased. The happy feast continued, and few people knew what had happened. But the disciples had seen a miracle, and they believed in Jesus.

JOHN

THE BETHESDA POOL

Some time later, Jesus travelled to Jerusalem to teach there and to cure people of diseases and sickness. While he was in the city, he went to a place called Bethesda, which had a special pool.

People who were sick came to the Bethesda pool and lay at its edge, waiting for the water to move. They believed that an angel of God came at certain times and stirred the water. When the water moved, the first person to step into the pool would be cured.

Walking in the crowd of sick people at Bethesda, Jesus came to a man who was paralyzed and could not move. Jesus knew that the man had been ill for a long time.

Jesus asked the man, "Do you want to be well?"

"Yes," the man answered. "But I have no one to put me into the pool when the water moves. I try to get there, but someone always reaches the water before me."

"Stand up," said Jesus. "Pick up your bed and walk."

At once the man stood up and was well again.

Jesus cured the paralyzed man on the Sabbath, the holy day of the Jewish week. When the Jewish leaders heard about the work Jesus had done on the Sabbath they were very angry. They believed no labor of any kind should be done on that day.

But Jesus said to them, "My Father in heaven is forever at work, and so am I."

JOHN

25

THE MAN
LOWERED THROUGH THE ROOF

Word began to spread through Judea and Galilee that Jesus was not only a great teacher but could cure people as well. After this the crowd of followers grew bigger than ever.

One day, Jesus was teaching in a house filled with listeners. Several people carrying a stretcher came to the house and tried to get in. On the stretcher was a man who was paralyzed. He could not walk. All he could do was lie in his bed all day long. His friends wanted to take him to Jesus to be cured.

When they could not get into the crowded house, the man's friends carried him up to the roof of the building. They pried off some of the roof tiles and made an opening. Then they carefully lowered the stretcher down through the roof until the man lay on the floor in front of Jesus.

Because they had worked so hard to reach him, Jesus knew that the sick man and his friends believed in him. But he did not heal the man's body at first. Instead he said, "Your sins are forgiven," to heal the man's soul.

Some of the people listening to Jesus were teachers of the ancient laws of Moses. What Jesus said made them angry. "No one can forgive sins but God!" they whispered to themselves.

Jesus knew their thoughts and knew that their hearts were turned against him. Still he continued. Jesus said to the paralyzed man, "Stand up. Take up your bed and go home."

The man who had been paralyzed rose to his feet. Everyone who saw him stand praised God. They were filled with wonder and said, "We have seen great things today."

LUKE

THE SERMON ON THE MOUNT

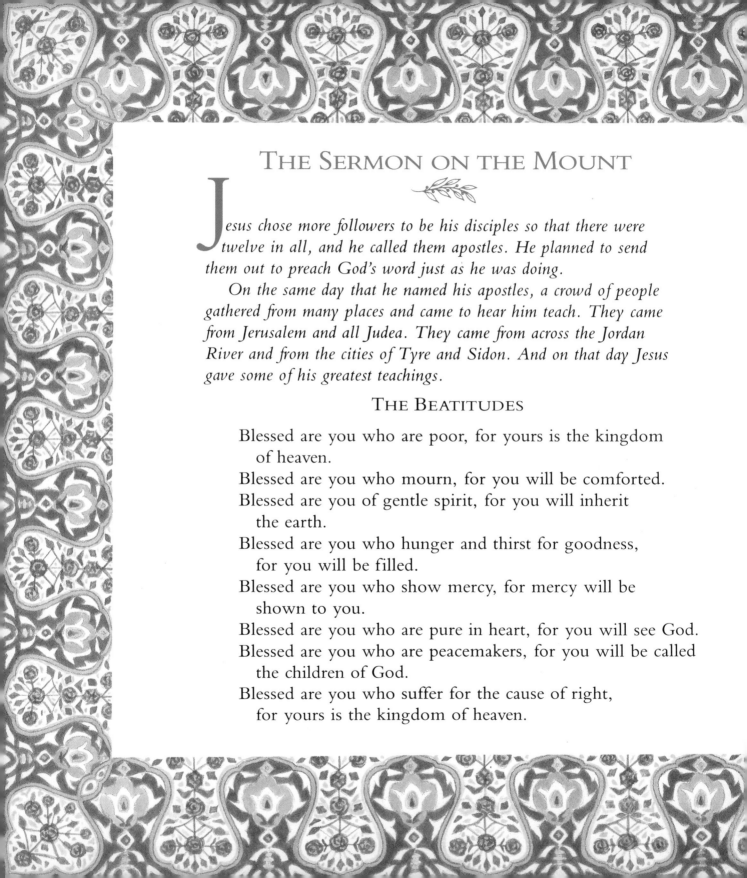

Jesus chose more followers to be his disciples so that there were twelve in all, and he called them apostles. He planned to send them out to preach God's word just as he was doing.

On the same day that he named his apostles, a crowd of people gathered from many places and came to hear him teach. They came from Jerusalem and all Judea. They came from across the Jordan River and from the cities of Tyre and Sidon. And on that day Jesus gave some of his greatest teachings.

THE BEATITUDES

Blessed are you who are poor, for yours is the kingdom of heaven.

Blessed are you who mourn, for you will be comforted.

Blessed are you of gentle spirit, for you will inherit the earth.

Blessed are you who hunger and thirst for goodness, for you will be filled.

Blessed are you who show mercy, for mercy will be shown to you.

Blessed are you who are pure in heart, for you will see God.

Blessed are you who are peacemakers, for you will be called the children of God.

Blessed are you who suffer for the cause of right, for yours is the kingdom of heaven.

THE LORD'S PRAYER

When you pray, do not pray in God's house only, where everyone can see you. Go into a room by yourself. Shut the door, and pray to God the Father who is unseen. And your Father will reward you.

And when you pray, say:

Our Father who art in heaven,
Hallowed be thy name.
Thy Kingdom come,
Thy will be done,
On earth as it is in heaven.
Give us this day our daily bread,
And forgive us our trespasses,
As we forgive those who trespass against us.
And lead us not into temptation,
But deliver us from evil.

For thine is the Kingdom and the power
And the glory, forever.

Amen.

THE LIGHT OF THE WORLD

You are the salt of the earth. You are the light of the world. But a candle that has been lit cannot be hidden. It is put in a candlestick and gives light to everyone in the house.

Let your light shine. Let it shine so brightly that those around you will see the good you do and praise your Father in heaven.

TURN THE OTHER CHEEK

In the days of old, men said, "An eye for an eye, and a tooth for a tooth." But I tell you: Do not hurt the man who wrongs you. If he slaps you on the right cheek, turn and offer him the left.

LOVE YOUR ENEMY

In the days of old, men said, "Love your neighbor, hate your enemy." But I tell you: Love your enemy. Bless those who speak badly of you. Pray for those who wish you harm. Do this so that you can truly be the children of your heavenly Father.

ASK AND YOU WILL RECEIVE

Ask, and you will receive. Seek, and you will find. Knock, and the door will be opened. For everyone who asks, receives. Those who seek, find. And the door is opened to those who knock.

BE READY FOR THE KINGDOM

Set your mind on God, and all the rest will come to you as well. Have no fear, little flock, for your Father has chosen to give you the kingdom. Only be ready.

THE GOLDEN RULE

Always treat others as you would like them to treat you.

MATTHEW and LUKE

CASTING THE FIRST STONE

One day when Jesus was in the temple in Jerusalem, an angry group of Pharisees approached him. The Pharisees were religious people who believed strongly in the laws of Moses. Some of the Pharisees hated Jesus because they thought he was teaching people to disobey the ancient laws.

The Pharisees who found Jesus in the temple that day had forced a woman to come with them. They stood her in front of Jesus. The woman, who was married, had not been faithful to her husband.

"Moses said that such a woman should be stoned," the Pharisees told Jesus. "What do you say?"

Jesus pretended that he did not hear them. He knew that the Pharisees were testing him, hoping he would break the law. Instead, Jesus leaned down and traced something on the ground with his fingers.

The Pharisees asked again, "What do you say about this woman?"

Finally Jesus sat up. He said to them, "If one of you is without sin, let him throw the first stone."

Slowly, one by one, the Pharisees quietly walked away. Not one of them could say he had never sinned. When Jesus and the woman were the only ones left, he spoke to her.

"Where are your accusers? Has no one stayed to condemn you?"

"No one, Master," answered the woman.

"Then I do not condemn you either," said Jesus. "Go now, and sin no more."

JOHN

THE PARABLE OF THE SOWER

This is a parable, or story, that Jesus told to teach a lesson.

A farmer went out to his fields to sow, or plant, seed.

Some of the seed that he threw fell on the path. It was stepped on and eaten by birds.

Some seed fell on rocks. It sprouted but the soil was shallow. The hot sun soon withered the sprouts because they had no roots.

Some seed fell among thistles. The prickly weeds grew with the seedlings and choked them.

But some of the seed fell on good soil. That seed grew well and produced a hundred times its worth.

When Jesus explained the story, he said the seed is the word of God. The soil is the different hearts and attitudes of people. Seeds that fall on the path are words that people hear but do not believe and are forgotten.

Seeds that fall on rocks are words that are heard with joy at first. People believe them for a short time but when these people are tempted, they desert God.

Seeds that fall among thistles are words that people hear, but they let themselves be distracted by the busy doings and worries of their lives. Their faith does not grow fully.

But the seeds that fall on good soil are those words received by people who listen with honest hearts. They understand the words and please God by their actions.

LUKE

35

THE DAUGHTER OF JAIRUS

One day in the town of Capernaum, one of the leaders of the synagogue was desperate to find Jesus. Jairus, as he was known, was very upset. When he found Jesus, he threw himself at Jesus' feet. "My daughter is dying," he cried. "I beg you to come and save her life."

Jesus and some of his apostles went with the man. As they walked through the town, a messenger from Jairus' house brought word that the child had died.

"Do not be afraid," Jesus said to Jairus. "Have faith." And they continued on to the house.

When they arrived, they found everyone in the house weeping and crying.

"Why do you weep?" Jesus asked. "The child is not dead. She is asleep."

But Jairus' family and friends did not believe Jesus and laughed at him. They knew the child was dead.

Jesus went into the room where the little girl lay. He held her hand. Then he said, "Get up, my child."

Immediately she got off the bed. She stood and even walked across the room. Jairus and his wife were filled with joy. And the story of the little girl who had been brought back to life spread all through the countryside.

MATTHEW, MARK, and LUKE

THE MIRACLE OF
THE LOAVES AND FISHES

More and more people became disciples of Jesus. Those who were sick in body or mind were cured and healed by Jesus' power. Others came to hear him teach. Jesus was almost never alone.

One day he and the apostles went by boat on the Sea of Galilee to find a quiet place on the far shore where they could be by themselves to get some rest. But word spread about their journey. When the boat came ashore, a crowd of about five thousand people were waiting for them.

When Jesus saw so many in need, his heart went out to them. They seemed like sheep without a shepherd to guide and protect them. So Jesus began teaching them many things.

By evening, everyone was growing hungry. A young boy who had brought some food offered it to the apostles. There were only five loaves of bread and two fish. Jesus said it would be enough food for everyone, but the apostles were puzzled. How could so little food feed such a large crowd?

Jesus took the bread and the fish and looked up to heaven. Then he blessed the food, broke the bread, and told the apostles to pass out all of it to the people. Jesus did the same with the fish.

The people ate as much as they wanted. Over and over the apostles reached into their baskets and gave out the food. When everyone had finished, Jesus told the apostles to gather up the food that had not been eaten. The apostles found enough bread left over to fill twelve large baskets.

MARK and JOHN

Jesus Walks on the Sea

When Jesus had fed the crowd of five thousand, the people who were there knew that he had performed a miracle. They said to each other excitedly, "Surely this is the Messiah."

That night Jesus went off by himself into the hillside to pray. The apostles decided to go by boat back to town. They climbed into their boat and pushed off.

While they were on the Sea of Galilee, a strong wind blew up. The sea grew rough. The apostles rowed hard. When they were out in the middle of the sea, they looked up from their rowing. Someone was walking toward them on top of the water. It was a frightening sight. "It is a ghost!" they said.

But it was Jesus walking toward the boat. He called to them and said, "Do not be afraid. It is I."

Then the apostle Peter said, "Lord, if it really is you, let me walk to you on the water."

"Come," said Jesus.

Peter stepped out of the boat onto the water. He walked a few steps toward Jesus. Then the wind blew and frightened him. As he grew afraid, he began to sink. "Save me, Lord," he cried.

Jesus quickly caught hold of Peter and took him to the boat. "Why did you hesitate?" Jesus asked him. "How little faith you have."

Astounded by what they had seen, the apostles said to Jesus, "Truly, you are the Son of God."

MATTHEW and JOHN

The Grain of Mustard Seed

One afternoon in the town where he was staying, Jesus saw a large group of people arguing on the street. In the group were several of his apostles.

When the crowd saw Jesus coming they grew quiet. One man stepped forward to speak to Jesus.

"I came to this town so that you could cure my son," the man said. "He is possessed by an evil spirit. When the spirit attacks him, my son cannot speak. He throws himself on the ground and grows rigid."

The man continued sadly, "Your disciples tried to help me but they could not. I beg you to make my son well."

"Bring him to me," said Jesus.

The boy was led to Jesus. The spirit grew violent in the presence of the Savior and threw the boy to the ground.

Jesus spoke to the spirit in a stern voice, saying, "Spirit, I command you to come out."

And the spirit came out. Afterward the boy lay on the ground as if he were dead. But Jesus took his hand, and the boy stood up.

Later the apostles asked Jesus why they had not been able to cure the child.

"Your faith was not strong enough," Jesus answered. "But I promise you that if your faith is only as big as a mustard seed, which is very small, it will be enough. Then you will be able to say to a mountain, 'Move. Go from this place to another.' And the mountain will move. Nothing will be impossible for you."

MATTHEW and MARK

LET THE CHILDREN COME

One day a large group of listeners around Jesus began leading children up to him so that he could bless them. The apostles did not think this was right and tried to turn the people away.

But Jesus said to his apostles, "Let the little children come to me. Do not stop them. The kingdom of God belongs to those who are like children. Anyone who cannot accept the kingdom of God as children do will never enter it."

And Jesus put his arms around the children. He laid his hands on them gently and blessed them.

On another day the apostles went to Jesus. "Who is the greatest in the kingdom of heaven?" they asked.

To answer, Jesus picked up a child and held him in his arms. "Let a person be as humble as this little one," he said, "and that person will be the greatest in the kingdom of God.

"Never look down on these little ones," Jesus continued. "I tell you they have guardian angels in heaven, angels who are forever in the presence of my heavenly Father."

MATTHEW and MARK

THE GOOD SAMARITAN

In his teachings, Jesus said each person must love his neighbor as much as himself.

One day a man listening to Jesus asked him, "Who is my neighbor?"

Jesus answered the man by telling this story:

A man was travelling on the lonely, winding road from Jerusalem to Jericho. A band of robbers attacked him. They took his money, beat him, and left him lying on the road half dead.

Soon a temple priest came down the road. When he saw the wounded man, he crossed to the other side and went on.

Then a man who was a member of the tribe of Levi came to the place where the man lay. The Levite also passed by and continued his journey.

But a man from Samaria came to the wounded man and did not pass by. He looked at the man and felt pity. He cleaned the man's wounds and bandaged them. Then the Samaritan put the wounded man onto his donkey and took him to an inn where he could rest.

That night the good Samaritan stayed with the man. The next morning, the Samaritan had to leave. But he gave the innkeeper some money and asked him to continue to take care of the man who had been hurt.

The Samaritan said to the innkeeper, "If you spend more than this, I will repay you when I come back."

When Jesus had finished telling the story, he put a question to the man who had been listening: "Of the three travellers on the road, which one was a neighbor to the wounded man?"

The man who had been listening said, "The one who showed mercy toward him."

Jesus said to the man, "Go and do the same."

LUKE

THE PRODIGAL SON

The Pharisees and teachers of the law often complained about the way Jesus taught. One day they began grumbling about the kind of people Jesus allowed to sit and listen to him. The Pharisees felt there were sinners of all kinds in the crowd.

To answer the Pharisees, Jesus told a story about a sinful son and a loving father. This is the story he told:

Once there was a wealthy farmer who had two sons. The younger son, who was a restless fellow, went to his father one day. "I want my share of the money that is to come to me," he said.

The father agreed to his request and gave the young man his share of the wealth. Once his son had the money, he left home and moved far away. In the years that followed, he spent money on foolish things until it was all gone.

Then a famine came to the land where the young man was living. By then he was so poor that he was nearly begging. At last he found a job as a farmhand, tending pigs. Unfortunately, he was paid so little that he was hungry all the time, so hungry he was tempted to eat the pig's food.

At last the young man realized what he had done. He said to himself, "I am starving. My father's servants have more to eat than I do. I will go home and tell my father I am sorry. I will say that I have done wrong and am not fit to be called his son anymore. I will ask only that my father take me back as one of his servants."

The young man made the long trip home. When his father saw him coming toward the house, the old man ran to meet him. He threw his arms around his son and hugged him. He told the servants to prepare a feast so that they could celebrate.

Later in the day, the older son returned from working in the fields. As he neared the house, he heard music and singing. A servant told him that his brother had come home and that his father had called for a celebration.

The older son was angry and would not go into the house. His father came outside and pleaded with him, but it was no use. The older son felt that he had always been more obedient and faithful than his brother. Even so, his father had never prepared a celebration in his honor.

"My boy," said the father, "you have been trustworthy and have stayed with me, and everything I have is yours. But how could we refuse to celebrate tonight? Your brother was dead and is alive again. Your brother was lost and has been found."

LUKE

THE MAN IN THE TREE

One day when Jesus and his apostles were travelling they came to the city of Jericho. People in the city knew Jesus was coming and lined the streets to see him.

One person in the crowd was a wealthy man named Zacchaeus, who was hated by his fellow Jews because he was a chief tax collector for the Romans.

Zacchaeus was a short man and could not see over the heads of the crowd as Jesus passed by. But Zacchaeus was determined to see Jesus, so he ran down the street ahead of the crowd. There he saw a sycamore tree and climbed up in its branches to make sure he had a good view.

Jesus walked down the road with the apostles until he came to the tree Zacchaeus had climbed. Then he looked up into the branches and said, "Come down quickly, Zacchaeus. I want to stay at your house."

The tax collector climbed down as fast as he could, his heart pounding. He led Jesus to his home and made him welcome. The people were shocked when they saw Jesus go to Zacchaeus' house. They said he was the guest of a sinner, a man who had cheated them when he collected their taxes.

While Jesus was in his house, the tax collector made a decision. He told Jesus that he would give away half of all he owned to the poor. "And if I have cheated anyone," he said, "I will give him four times the amount."

Jesus was pleased with the decision Zacchaeus had made. And on that day Zacchaeus became a follower of Jesus.

LUKE

53

RAISING LAZARUS

Among the people who loved Jesus and believed in him were two sisters named Mary and Martha, and their brother Lazarus. These three lived in a village called Bethany, close to Jerusalem.

One day Jesus received sad news. His friend Lazarus had died. Jesus made the trip to Bethany and arrived there four days after Lazarus' death.

When he saw Martha he said, "Your brother will rise again." Then he went to the cave that had become Lazarus' tomb. Mary and Martha went with him, and so did the friends who had come to comfort them after their brother's death.

Jesus asked that the big stone in front of the cave be dragged away. Then he stood at the entrance and looked up to heaven. "Father, I thank you," he said, "for I know that you hear me."

Then he cried out in a loud voice, "Lazarus, come out!" As the crowd watched, someone wrapped in burial cloths walked out of the cave. "Take off his grave clothes and let him go," Jesus said. They took the wrappings off, and saw it was Lazarus.

These are the words Jesus spoke in Bethany: "Whoever believes in me shall never die but shall have everlasting life."

JOHN

JESUS IS ANOINTED

Jesus began his last journey to Jerusalem. On the way, he told the apostles what would happen to him there. "I will be arrested by the priests and by those who guard the laws," he said. "Then I will be tried, sentenced, and put to death on a cross. On the third day after my death, I will rise again."

The apostles heard what Jesus said, but they did not believe him.

It was six days before the Passover festival. Friends honored Jesus with a special supper. One of the people who came that night to be with Jesus was Mary, the sister of Lazarus. Mary brought sweet-smelling oil and poured it on the feet of Jesus. She smoothed on the oil with her long hair, and the house was filled with a fragrant smell.

Judas Iscariot, one of the apostles, accused Mary of wasting expensive perfume. "We should have sold the oil," he told her, "and given the money to the poor."

"Let her be," said Jesus. "You will always have the poor to care for, but I will not always be with you."

Soon after this, Judas met secretly with the chief priests in Jerusalem and offered to help them arrest Jesus.

LUKE and JOHN

JESUS ENTERS JERUSALEM

The next day Jesus came to the city of Jerusalem. But before he entered the city, he stopped near a village just outside.

"Go into the village," he told two of the apostles. "You will find a donkey tied there. Bring it to me."

Then Jesus said, "If anyone asks you why you are taking the donkey, tell him the Lord has need of it. That person will understand."

The apostles did what Jesus told them to do and found the donkey and returned with it.

In that way a prophecy was fulfilled. The prophets of old had said that a Savior would come to lead Israel, a gentle king who would enter Jerusalem riding on a donkey, the beast of burden.

Jesus did enter the city riding on a donkey. His apostles walked at his side. A joyful crowd of believers went ahead of him, and others came behind.

Excited people lined the road into the old walled city. To honor Jesus as he passed, they laid their coats on the pavement. Others cut branches from palm trees, and they spread these in his path.

The city was wild with joy. People everywhere shouted, "Hosanna to the Son of David! Hosanna in the heavens! Blessed is he who comes in the name of God."

MATTHEW, MARK, and JOHN

Driving the Merchants from the Temple

After Jesus entered Jerusalem, he went to the great temple. Before going inside, he stood in the temple courtyard and saw many merchants who were doing business there. They were selling pigeons, sheep, and even cattle. The animals were sold at high prices to worshippers who wanted them for sacrifices to God. There were also moneychangers seated at tables, and they did not always do business honestly.

Jesus saw that the courtyard had been turned into a marketplace and was very angry. He made a small whip with lengths of rope and began driving the merchants and their animals out of the courtyard. He upset the moneychangers' tables, and their coins rolled to the ground.

Then Jesus began to speak to the crowd that had gathered. He reminded them of the words of the scriptures. "It is written that the house of God shall be a house of prayer for all people," he said angrily. "But I say you have turned it into a den of thieves."

Some of the chief priests and men of the law saw Jesus drive the merchants away and hated him even more than before. They hated him because people listened to him as if they were spellbound. The priests hated Jesus because they were losing more and more followers to him. And the angry priests began to plot Jesus' death.

MARK and JOHN

THE LAST SUPPER

It was almost time for the Passover holiday. The apostles found a large upstairs room in a house in Jerusalem and prepared a Passover supper.

When evening came Jesus sat at a big table with all twelve apostles. He said to them, "This is the last meal I will share with you before my death."

Then he took some bread and thanked God for it. He broke the bread into pieces and gave it to the apostles. He said to them, "Take this and eat. This is my body which is given for you. Do this in remembrance of me."

Then he took a cup of wine and thanked God for it. "Drink from this cup," he told the apostles. "This is my blood, which will be shed for you and for many, for the forgiveness of sins."

During the meal, Jesus told the apostles that someone at the table would turn against him. "One of you," he said, "will betray me."

They all seemed bewildered and upset by the news and asked who would do this terrible thing. Jesus turned to Judas and said, "Go quickly. Do what you have to do." No one else at the table understood that Jesus was speaking to the one who would betray him. Judas got up from the table and left.

After supper, Jesus rose from the table and went to find a towel and a basin. He poured water in the basin and began to wash the apostles' feet.

But Peter would not let Jesus wash his feet. He did not think it was right for his Lord to do such a thing.

Jesus said to Peter, "If I do not wash you, you will not be one of mine."

Then Peter understood and asked him to wash not only his feet but also his hands and face. Jesus said that it was enough to wash Peter's feet.

When Jesus had finished, he began to speak and to teach the apostles for the last time. "I will not be with you much longer," he said. "Now is the time for me to give you a new commandment: Love one another. As I have loved you, so you must love each other. By that love, people will know you are my disciples."

And Jesus said, "Where I am going, you cannot follow now. But do not worry. Trust in God always, and trust in me. There are many rooms in my Father's house. I go to prepare a place for you when you come."

Then the apostle Thomas grew frightened. "Lord, we do not know where you are going," he said. "How then will we find the way?"

"I am the way," said Jesus. "I am the truth and the life. The one who loves me will be loved by my Father."

The hour grew late. It was time to go. Jesus blessed the apostles and said, "Believe in me, and you will know peace. The world is filled with trouble and hardship, but take courage. I have overcome the world."

MATTHEW, LUKE, and JOHN

IN THE GARDEN OF GETHSEMANE

After the Passover supper, when it was late at night, the apostles walked with Jesus to a quiet garden called Gethsemane, on the Mount of Olives. They knew they would not be together much longer.

Jesus said to them, "As it is written in the scriptures, you will desert me tonight. But when I have risen again, I will be with you in Galilee."

The apostles did not believe Jesus. Peter said, "Master, everyone else may desert you, but I never will."

"Before the cock crows at dawn," Jesus answered, "you will deny three times that you even know me."

Jesus went to pray and took only Peter, James, and John with him. Anguish and sorrow overwhelmed Jesus. "My heart is ready to break with grief," he said to the three apostles. "Wait for me here."

Jesus went on a little farther to be alone to pray. He threw himself on the ground and asked for God's help. "Father," he cried aloud, "if it can be, let this cup pass me by. And yet, let it be your will and not mine." Jesus went on praying for a long time.

Then an angel from heaven appeared and gave him strength. He prayed again, with all his heart.

When Jesus finished praying, he was not in torment any longer. He went back to Peter, James, and John and was sad to find them sleeping. He woke them and said, "Rise now. The time has come when I will be betrayed."

Then the garden of Gethsemane was filled with soldiers. They came carrying torches and were armed with swords. The soldiers had been sent by the temple priests and the Pharisees to arrest Jesus. Leading them was the apostle named Judas, who was the traitor.

Judas went up to Jesus and greeted him and kissed him on the cheek. This was the sign the soldiers had been told to watch for. They seized Jesus and held him.

At that moment Peter drew a sword and slashed out at one of the servants of the High Priest, cutting off his ear.

But Jesus said to Peter, "Put your sword away. Those who live by the sword also die by it. My Father would send twelve legions of angels to help. But how would the words of the prophets be fulfilled that say these things must happen?"

Jesus healed the man who had been wounded. Then he turned to the soldiers. "I am the one you want," he said. "Let the others go."

As Jesus was taken out of the garden, the frightened apostles drew back into the darkness and ran away.

MATTHEW, LUKE, and JOHN

PETER DENIES KNOWING CHRIST

Even though it was the middle of the night, the soldiers took Jesus to the palace of the High Priest to be tried. Peter followed them, but only at a safe distance.

In the courtyard of the palace, the servants had lit a fire to take the chill from the night air. Peter came and sat near the fire. A palace servant recognized him and said to the others, "This man was with Jesus."

Peter denied it, saying, "I do not know him."

Later someone else saw Peter and claimed he was one of Jesus' followers. Again Peter denied it.

Finally a third person recognized Peter by his voice and said, "Of course this man was with Jesus. I can tell by his accent. He is a Galilean."

"I do not know what you are talking about," said Peter angrily. But at that moment, he heard a cock crowing in the distance. He remembered Jesus' words: "Before the cock crows, you will deny me three times."

Peter turned. There, in the distance, he saw Jesus looking at him. Then Peter left the courtyard and wept bitterly.

That night the men who were guarding Jesus mocked him and beat him. They blindfolded him and slapped him, saying, "If you are a prophet, tell us who hit you." But Jesus chose not to answer them.

LUKE

Jesus Before Pontius Pilate

By the time morning came, the High Priest and temple elders had condemned Jesus to death in a court trial. They said he claimed to be the Messiah, the Savior, which was a sin against God.

Judas, the apostle who had betrayed Jesus, learned that the court had condemned Jesus to death. Then Judas felt terrible sorrow for what he had done. He gave back the money he had been paid to betray Jesus, but the weight of his sin was still more than he could bear. In despair, Judas went away and hanged himself.

After they condemned him, the members of the court took Jesus to Pontius Pilate. Pilate was the Roman governor in Jerusalem. Only the Roman governor could have Jesus executed. The court members asked Pilate to put Jesus to death for his crimes. They said he called himself a king over the Jews, which was treason against Rome.

Inside his headquarters, Pilate questioned Jesus. "Are you king of the Jews?" he asked.

"My kingdom does not belong to this world," Jesus replied.

"Are you a king then?" Pilate asked.

"You say that I am," Jesus answered.

At last Pilate went outside and spoke to the crowd waiting for his decision. "I can find no fault in him," Pilate announced.

But many of the priests and religious leaders hated Jesus and called for his death. "Crucify him, crucify him." This stirred up the crowd and they began to shout, too.

Then Pilate remembered a Passover custom. At the time of the feast, the Roman governor could let one prisoner go free. The people were allowed to choose which one it would be.

Now Barabbas, a prisoner whose name was known to everyone, was a robber and murderer. Pilate spoke to the crowd. "Which prisoner shall I release?" he cried. "Barabbas, or Jesus, king of the Jews?"

"Not Jesus!" they shouted. "Barabbas!"

Then Pilate asked what he should do with Jesus. Again the angry crowd shouted, "Crucify him!"

Feeling he could do nothing more, Pilate called for a bowl of water and washed his hands as a sign that he was not guilty of Jesus' death. Then he freed the murderer Barabbas.

After that Pilate told his soldiers to take Jesus and whip him. They also made a crown for him out of branches covered with thorns. The soldiers put the crown on his head and laughed and said, "Hail, king of the Jews!"

Then Pilate showed the crowd that Jesus had been punished, but they were not satisfied. They shouted, "Take him away! Crucify him!"

Pilate tried to talk to Jesus again, but Jesus would not answer. Finally Pilate said to him, "Do you not see that I have the power to let you go or crucify you?"

"You have no power over me at all," Jesus said, "except the power granted to you by God."

Still filled with doubts, Pilate handed Jesus over to his own soldiers to be crucified.

MATTHEW and JOHN

THE CRUCIFIXION

A crowd walked with Jesus through the streets of Jerusalem to a hill called Golgotha, which means "place of the skull." The soldiers pulled a man named Simon out of the crowd and forced him to carry the heavy wooden cross for Jesus.

When they reached Golgotha, the soldiers put Jesus on the cross, nailing his feet and hands.

In terrible pain, Jesus looked up to heaven and said, "Father, forgive them, for they know not what they do."

While they waited for him to die, the soldiers drew lots to see who would get his clothes. They made fun of Jesus and laughed at the sign that had been put over his head. The sign said, "This is the king of the Jews."

Two criminals were crucified with Jesus, one on his right and the other on his left. "If you are the Savior," said one criminal, "why don't you save yourself and us?"

But the other criminal believed that Jesus was not guilty, and fearing God he said to him, "Remember me when you come to your kingdom."

Jesus answered, saying, "Today you will be with me in Paradise."

Suddenly the sun stopped shining and the sky over the city was dark for three hours. At last Jesus cried, "Father, into your hands I commit my spirit."

After Jesus said this, he died.

LUKE

THE TOMB IS SEALED

One of Jesus' followers was a man named Joseph, a member of the Jewish council. He had not agreed to Jesus' crucifixion. Soon after the death of Jesus, Joseph dared to go to the governor, Pontius Pilate, and ask for Jesus' body.

Pilate gave permission, and Joseph took the body down from the cross. He wrapped it with sweet spices in a soft linen sheet and laid it in a new tomb cut out of rock. A large stone was rolled in front of the tomb.

It was Friday, late in the afternoon. The Sabbath was about to begin. Until the Sabbath was over, everyone would rest.

LUKE

CHRIST IS RISEN

Early on Sunday morning, Mary Magdalene went to the tomb where Jesus had been buried. Mary was one of the women from Galilee who had followed Jesus to Jerusalem. When she reached the tomb, Mary saw that the stone had been rolled away.

Mary looked in the tomb and saw that the body of her Lord was no longer there. Mary grew frightened. She ran to tell the apostles that the tomb was empty.

80

Two apostles, Peter and another, came back to the tomb with Mary. They saw that the linen wrappings used for the burial were lying there neatly folded, but that the body of Jesus was gone. And when they saw these things, they believed Jesus had risen from the dead.

The apostles went to tell the others what had happened, but Mary stayed at the tomb. She peered inside, and there she saw two angels, all white and shining. They were sitting where the body of Jesus had been, one at the head and one at the foot.

"Why are you weeping?" the angels asked Mary.

"They have taken my Lord away," she answered, "and I do not know where they have laid him."

She turned around as if to look for Jesus and saw a man standing near her. It was Jesus, but Mary did not recognize him in the dim light. She thought he was a gardener.

"Woman, why are you crying?" the man asked. "Who is it you are looking for?"

"Oh, sir," said Mary, "if you have taken Jesus away, tell me where you have laid him."

The man said quietly, "Mary."

Then she knew it was Jesus. "Master," she answered.

"Go to my brothers," said Jesus, "and tell them I am going to the one who is God the Father."

Then Mary went to the apostles and said joyfully, "I have seen him. I have seen the Lord."

LUKE and JOHN

Jesus Appears to the Apostles

On the same day that Mary Magdalene went to the tomb, some of the apostles were gathered together in a house in Jerusalem to talk among themselves. Because Judas was dead, there were only eleven apostles.

Suddenly Jesus was in the room with them. "Peace be with you," he said. Then he showed them his wounds. The apostles saw that it was indeed Jesus and they were filled with joy. They were together again. Jesus talked with the men he most loved.

When he was gone, the apostles realized that Thomas, one of the eleven, had not been there. When Thomas returned, the others told him excitedly that they had seen the Lord.

But Thomas doubted it was true. "Unless I see the mark of the nails on his hands and touch his side," he said, "I will not believe he was here."

One week later, when the apostles were together in the same room, Jesus appeared among them again. "Peace be with you," he said.

This time Thomas was there, too. Jesus turned to him and said, "Look at my hands. Reach out and touch my side. Do not doubt anymore."

Thomas saw the wounds on Jesus and said, "My Lord and my God."

Then Jesus said to Thomas, "You believe in me because you have seen me. Blessed are those who have never seen me and yet believe in me."

JOHN

Jesus and the Miraculous Catch of Fish

After Jesus had risen from the dead, the apostles went back to Galilee as he had told them to do.

While they were staying in a town by the Sea of Galilee, some of them decided to go out fishing one night. They worked hard, but when morning came they had caught nothing.

As the apostles headed the boat back to shore, they saw a man on the beach. The apostles did not know it, but the man was Jesus.

He called to the fishermen, "Throw out your net on the right side of the boat." They did and suddenly the net was full of fish.

Then John said, "It is the Lord."

Peter knew John was right and eagerly jumped into the sea, wanting to swim to shore. The others brought the boat in, towing the net full of fish.

When they reached the shore the apostles saw that Jesus had already made a good fire. "Bring some of the fish you have caught," he said.

Peter went back and dragged the net ashore. When the apostles counted their catch, they found one hundred and fifty-three large fish. And in spite of the weight of the huge catch, the net had not ripped.

"Come and eat breakfast," said Jesus.

This was the third time Jesus appeared to the apostles.

JOHN

JESUS SAYS FAREWELL

Forty days after the death of Jesus, also called "the Christ," he was ready to be taken up into heaven. He appeared to the apostles one last time and told them what to do.

"Stay in Jerusalem until you are armed with power from above," he said. "You are the witnesses to all that has happened, and you will receive the gift promised by my Father. Soon you will be baptized with the Holy Spirit."

Then he said to them, "After that time, go and make all nations my disciples. Baptize people everywhere in the name of the Father and the Son and the Holy Spirit. Teach them all I have told to you. And know that I am with you always, even to the end of time."

When Jesus had finished speaking, he walked with the apostles until they were out of the city. He went with them as far as the fields near Bethany. There Jesus stopped and turned to the friends he loved. He reached out to bless them, and blessing them, he was lifted up into heaven.

Afterward, the apostles felt a great joy inside themselves. They went back to Jerusalem, praising God again and again.

MATTHEW, LUKE, and ACTS

THE APOSTLES CARRY ON

After Christ rose up into heaven, the apostles stayed in Jerusalem as he had told them to do. To replace Judas, they chose a follower named Matthias, who had been with them from the beginning.

Pentecost came, a feast celebrating the first fruits of the harvest. On this day the apostles were gathered together in a house, praying to the Lord. Suddenly they heard a strange and wonderful sound all through the house. The sound was like a great rushing wind, and it came from heaven.

Then what seemed to be a tiny flame of fire came to rest on each of the apostles, and each was filled with the Holy Spirit.

From that day on, the apostles began to teach in the name of Jesus Christ, the Son of God. Peter, along with the other apostles, preached about Jesus. Many accepted the new promise of the kingdom of God and many were baptized in the name of Christ.

The people who followed the teachings of Christ shared a common life in Jerusalem. They wanted to be together to hear the apostles speak, to break bread, and to pray. They shared everything they had together. Sometimes they sold what they owned and used the money for the good of all. Faith in Jesus drew them together, and they loved each other.

Every day the Lord blessed them and new followers joined their numbers.

ACTS

ON THE ROAD TO DAMASCUS

In Jerusalem at that time there were some rigid religious leaders who wanted to stop the growth of the followers of Christ. One of these was a teacher of the Hebrew law named Saul. Saul felt it was his holy duty to hunt down people who followed the teachings of Christ and have them put in prison.

Soon Saul decided to go outside of Jerusalem to search for followers. The first city he went to was Damascus. In his pocket were letters from the Jewish council in Jerusalem giving him power to arrest any followers of Christ he found.

While Saul was on the road to Damascus, the sky around him suddenly filled with light. Saul fell to the ground. He heard a voice say, "Saul, why are you trying to go against me?"

Saul was shaken and bewildered. "Who are you?" he asked.

The voice answered, "I am Jesus, the one you are hurting. Get up now. Go into the city. There you will be told what to do next."

Saul stood up. But when he looked around, he could not see. The men who were travelling with him had to lead him to Damascus.

Saul was blind for three days. During that time he came to believe in Jesus as the Son of God. A follower of Christ named Ananias came to Saul and, with God's power, helped Saul to see again. Then he was baptized for the forgiveness of his sins. Paul, as he later came to be known, eventually returned to Jerusalem, and became a great minister of Christ's teachings, a man chosen by God to bring the name of the Lord to many nations.

ACTS

91

PETER IN PRISON

The number of people who followed the teachings of Christ continued to grow. The Roman government in Jerusalem began to resent the new religion and attacked its followers whom they called Christians. They arrested James, one of the twelve apostles, and put him to death with a sword. Then Roman soldiers went to find the apostle Peter and threw him into prison. The followers of Jesus prayed for Peter day and night while he was in a prison.

In his cell one night, Peter awoke suddenly. Before him stood an angel of the Lord. The cell blazed with light. The chains that had held Peter's wrists fell to the floor.

"Get up. Get dressed and follow me," said the angel. Peter thought he was dreaming, but he and the angel hurried past the cell guards, through prison gates that opened by themselves, and out into the dark streets of the city.

When the angel was gone, Peter made his way to a house where he knew people had been praying for him. After he knocked, a young woman came and asked through the closed door, "Who is there?"

Peter identified himself. When the young woman heard his voice, she was so overjoyed that she forgot to open the door but ran instead to tell the others in the house.

When they finally let Peter in, everyone was amazed to see him. Peter told them what had happened and how the Lord had brought him out of prison.

ACTS

A Vision of the Kingdom of God

There was a follower of Christ named John. John was a prisoner of the Romans for many years because of his beliefs. While he was a prisoner, he had a vision of what heaven would be like. In the true belief that his vision was from God, John wrote down everything that happened. Here are some things he wrote:

"I saw a new heaven and a new earth. And I heard a voice out of heaven, saying, 'God dwells among men, and they shall be his people. And he will wipe every tear from their eyes. There will be an end to death and to mourning, to crying and to pain. For the old order has passed away!'

"And I saw the holy city of Jerusalem coming down out of heaven. It shone with the glory of God. It radiated like a priceless jewel, like jasper. It had a great high wall with twelve gates, and at every gate stood an angel of God. The city was made of pure gold, bright as flawless crystal.

"I saw no temple in the city, for the Lord God Almighty and the Lamb of God were there to be worshipped. And the city had no need of sun or moon, for the glory of God brightened it and the Lamb of God was its light.

"And all who are servants of the Lord shall worship him there and see his face, and they will live with him forever."

THE REVELATION OF JOHN

And Jesus said:

I have come that men and women may have life and may have it in all its fullness.

I am the good shepherd. The good shepherd calls his sheep by name and leads them, and the sheep follow because they know him.

I am the good shepherd. To my beloved sheep I give eternal life. They shall not perish, and no one will ever take them from my care.

JOHN